# VOLLEYBALL DEFENSES

In the dynamic world of volleyball, the game is not just about powerful spikes and perfect sets; it's a strategic battle where defense plays a pivotal role. From the precision of a well-executed perimeter defense to the intricacies of a hybrid system, understanding the various types of volleyball defenses is like unlocking a treasure trove of strategic possibilities.

In this book, we embark on an exploration of the multifaceted realm of volleyball defenses. We dive deep into the intricacies of the perimeter defense, the precision of rotation, the agility of

# VOLLEYBALL DEFENSES

man-up formations, the adaptability of middle-middle structures, and the innovation of hybrid systems. As we journey through each of these defensive strategies, we will uncover their unique strengths, applications, and the tactical thinking that makes them essential in the modern game of volleyball.

For players, coaches, and enthusiasts alike, this book offers a comprehensive guide to not just understanding these defenses but also mastering them. Whether you're a novice looking to grasp the fundamentals or an experienced player seeking to fine-tune

# VOLLEYBALL DEFENSES

your defensive skills, the pages that follow are your roadmap to defensive excellence in the world of volleyball. So, join us on this enlightening expedition as we delve into the various types of volleyball defenses, where every page unfolds a new layer of the game's strategic beauty..

# A LIST OF SOME ...

# VOLLEYBALL DEFENSES

"PERIMETER"

"PERIMETER HYBRID"

"ROTATION"

"COUNTER ROTATION"

"MAN UP"

"MIDDLE MIDDLE"

"HYBRID"

# VOLLEYBALL DEFENSES

## WHICH DEFENSE?

When it comes to deciding on a defense, a crucial realization is that it's not always about stopping every attack your opponents throw at you; it's about making calculated decisions as a team. You'll find that there are attacks you can take away with a well-executed defense, but in doing so, you might concede openings in other areas. It's a strategic dance, a give-and-take, where the team must assess their strengths and the opponent's

# VOLLEYBALL
## DEFENSES

### WHICH DEFENSE?

weaknesses, adapting their defensive formations and tactics accordingly. Let's look at this Rotation Defense scenerio:

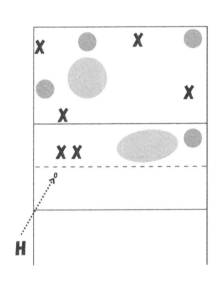

The red spots are hard hits and orange are shots. Here are some of the holes in the rotation defense against an Outside hitter.

Rotation is good against tips & taking the typical shots like cross away, but every defense has their weaknesses.

# KEY CONCEPTS: SEEMS

One of the key concepts of the backrow defense is who's ball is it and who has what on the seem?:

**image 1**     **image 2**

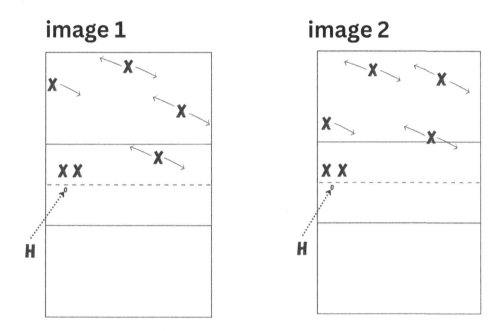

In this example, it's typical for middle back to cover behind and the corners, but if you are blocking line and middle back moves over into the seem of the block in image 2, then you might have to make some adjustments on who has what seem.

# KEY CONCEPTS: READING

The next key concept is reading around the block to set up your back row defense.

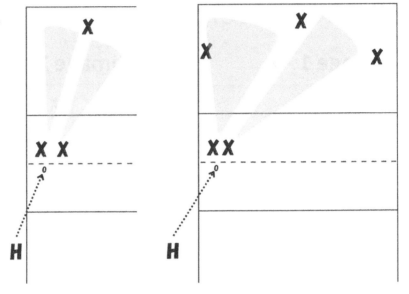

The key is for any back row defender is to move to their defensive position and stop before the hitter makes contact. As far as position, you never what to be behind the block, as you want to be able to see the hitter and get around the block as those are the hard hits and you want to be in position before they are hit.

# KEY CONCEPTS: BLOCKING

The next key concept is blocking (line, cross, and ball).

**Blocking against a Outside hitter. :**

| line | cross | ball |
|:---:|:---:|:---:|
|  |  |  |

**Blocking against a typical Rightside hitter. :**

| line | cross | ball |
|:---:|:---:|:---:|
|  |  |  |

For blocking line, make sure you place your hand on the inside of the court to the ball. For cross, your outside hand should be on the ball. And for ball, both hands should be on the ball.

# PERIMETER

## VOLLEYBALL
## DEFENSE

# WHAT IS A PERIMETER DEFENSE?

A volleyball perimeter defense is a backcourt defensive formation where three players align near the back boundary of the court, while the other three are at the net and the off blocker drops back to the perimeter as well. It is used to guard against powerful attacks from deep-court hitters, providing effective coverage for the back row. This formation allows the back-row players to dig and control incoming attacks, facilitating smooth transitions to offensive plays.

# PERIMETER
## VOLLEYBALL
### DEFENSE

## ADVANTAGES

1. Effective Against Deep Attacks: It is particularly effective in guarding against powerful and deep attacks from the opposing team. Back-row players are strategically positioned to receive and control these hits.

2. Coverage of Backcourt: Perimeter defense provides extensive coverage of the backcourt, making it harder for the opposing team to find open spaces for their shots.

3. Smooth Transition to Offense: Successful defensive plays in the perimeter defense allow for quick transitions to offense, as the back-row players can set the ball to their teammates at the net.

# PERIMETER
## VOLLEYBALL
### DEFENSE

## ADVANTAGES (CONT.)

4. Adaptable: This defense can adapt to various types of attacks, including both strong attacks and deep shots.

5. Teamwork and Communication: It encourages teamwork and communication among players in the back row, as they must coordinate to cover different zones effectively.

6. Suitable for All Skill Levels: The perimeter defense is suitable for players of all skill levels, making it a fundamental and versatile defensive strategy in volleyball.

# PERIMETER
## VOLLEYBALL
### DEFENSE

## DISADVANTAGES

1.Vulnerability to Short Shots: One of the main weaknesses is its vulnerability to short shots and dinks. The back-row players may struggle to cover the area close to the net, making them susceptible to well-placed tips and roll shots.

2. Dependency on Back-Row Players: The effectiveness of a perimeter defense heavily relies on the skills and positioning of the back-row players, which can be a disadvantage if they are not strong defensively.

# PERIMETER
## VOLLEYBALL
### DEFENSE

## DISADVANTAGES (CONT.)

3. Can Be Predictable: Skilled opponents might predict the areas that the back-row players are likely to defend, potentially making it easier for them to exploit gaps.

# PERIMETER DEFENSE

## Base (standard lineup):

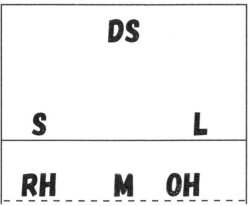

We are going to start in a standard base with setter back row. Don't release from base until the ball leaves the setters hands.

## Defense against...

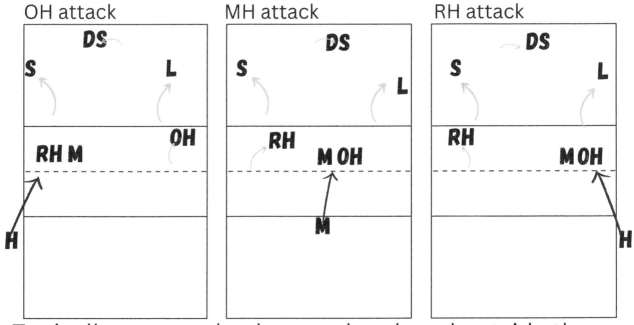

Typically we want backrow to be placed outside the block & between the block. If the block is closed then instead of between the block, then BR can read. Usually never behind the block.

# PERIMETER HYBRID

# VOLLEYBALL DEFENSE

# WHAT IS A PERIMETER HYBRID DEFENSE?

In a volleyball perimeter hybrid defense with the off blocker picking up tips, the back-row players are strategically positioned near the back boundary of the court to guard against deep attacks. The off blocker, typically one of the front-row players, is responsible for reading and reacting to "tips" or short, finesse shots executed by the opposing team. This defensive formation ensures that both powerful hits and subtle tips are accounted for, allowing the team to maintain effective coverage of the backcourt.

# PERIMETER HYBRID
## VOLLEYBALL
### DEFENSE

## ADVANTAGES

1. Effective Against Short Shots: The presence of the off blocker in the front row enhances the defense's ability to handle short and finesse shots like tips, dumps, and roll shots effectively.

2. Balanced Front and Back Coverage: This defense provides a balanced approach by combining the strengths of perimeter back-row defense with added coverage near the net, making it adaptable to various attack types.

3. Seamless Transition to Offense: With a front-row player prepared to defend against tips, quick transitions from defense to offense are facilitated, as they can use their position to set up offensive plays.

# ADVANTAGES (CONT.)

4. Diverse Defensive Options: The off blocker can contribute to both blocking and digging, adding versatility to the defense and making it effective against different attacking styles.

5. Reduced Vulnerability to Short Attacks: The combination of back-row and front-row players reduces the vulnerability to short attacks, as there's a player strategically placed to defend against them.

6. Improved Net Presence: Having a front-row player ready to pick up tips or block attacks can increase the team's overall presence at the net, making it harder for the opposing team to execute effective offensive plays.

# PERIMETER HYBRID
## VOLLEYBALL
### DEFENSE

# DISADVANTAGES

1. Holes in Defense: The off blocker's transition from the front row to the back row may leave gaps in the defense, especially around their base.

2. Increased Pressure on Back-Row Players: The back-row players, including the off blocker transitioning to the back row, face increased pressure to cover both deep shots and holes around the off blocker's base.

3. Dependence on the Off Blocker's Skill: The effectiveness of this defense relies heavily on the off blocker's ability to read the game, anticipate attacks, and react swiftly.

# DISADVANTAGES (CONT.)

4. Transition Challenges: The transition from a off blocking position to transitional attacking position for the off blocker after picking up a tip can be intricate and may not always be executed seamlessly, leaving 1 less hitter.

5. Potential for Miscommunication: Defending shots in the vicinity of the off blocker's base may require clear communication between players to avoid overlaps or gaps.

6. Predictability: Skilled opponents may recognize that shots are likely to target the off blocker's base in this defense.

# PERIMETER HYBRID DEFENSE

## Base (standard lineup):

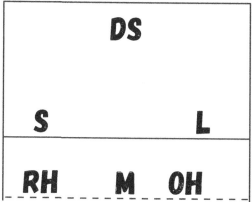

We are going to start in a standard base with setter back row. Don't release from base until the ball leaves the setters hands. The off blockers will move in more for tips in this defense.

## Defense against...

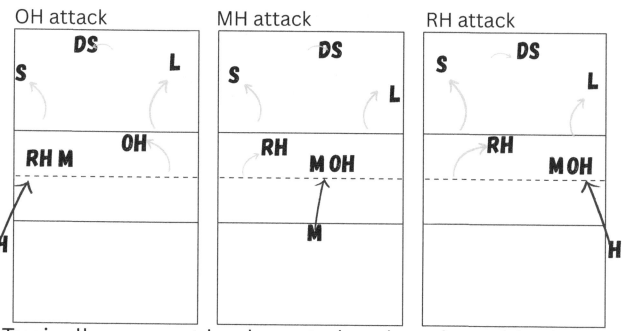

Typically we want backrow to be placed outside the block & between the block. If the block is closed then instead of between the block, then BR can read. Usually never behind the block.

# ROTATION

## VOLLEYBALL
### DEFENSE

# WHAT IS A ROTATION DEFENSE?

A volleyball rotation defense is a dynamic defensive formation employed by teams during the opponent's attack. It involves players shifting positions in a counter clockwise manner, with each player occupying a specific rotation spot on the court. This strategic rotation allows teams to maintain proper court coverage, adapt to the picking up tips and off shots, and prepare for subsequent plays.

In this example we are going to just rotate against the outside hitter which is the most common way to run rotation. That way your left back Libero is still in digging position against both pins.

# ROTATION

## VOLLEYBALL DEFENSE

## ADVANTAGES

1. Effective Blocking: Rotation defense excels in blocking at the net as blocking CROSS is highly efficient and easier to close.

2. Tip coverage: Able to pick up tips more efficiently against OH as it pulls someone (right back up for tips right away).

3. Effective Coverage: It provides good coverage against typical hit balls as it puts the best defenders in those coverage spots (line, cross, and cut).

4. Hide Bad defenders: If you have a setter that is poor at defense, then you can pull her up for tips instead.

# ROTATION
## VOLLEYBALL
### DEFENSE

## DISADVANTAGES

1. Spreads the defense: Rotation defense can be susceptible to hard hits over the block as the backrow is spread out and their are bigger holes.

2. Out of system: The defense tends to put your team out of system on tips from OH attack as the setter will take the first contact.

3. Energy Demanding: As players have to mover over long distances more often to get into position as middle back is always moving to the line. Susceptible to quick sets.

# ROTATION DEFENSE

## Base (standard lineup):

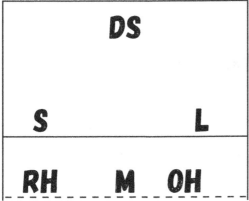

We are going to start in a standard base with setter back row. Don't release from base until the ball leaves the setters hands. Back row and off blocker rotates into position. In this example we are only rotating against OH.

## Defense against...

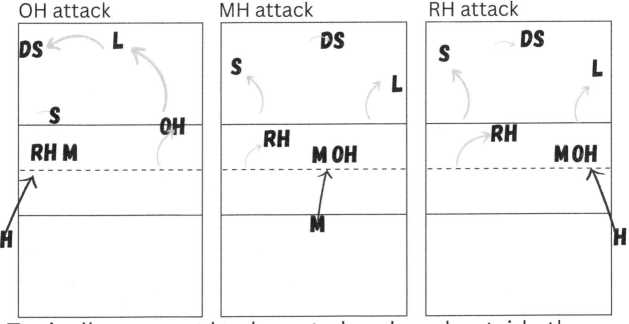

Typically we want backrow to be placed outside the block & between the block. If the block is closed then instead of between the block, then BR can read. Usually never behind the block.

# COUNTER ROTATION

## VOLLEYBALL DEFENSE

# WHAT IS A COUNTER ROTATION DEFENSE?

A volleyball counter rotation defense is a dynamic defensive formation employed by teams during the opponent's attack. It involves players shifting positions in a clockwise manner when the outside hitter attacks and counter clockwise when the right side hitter attacks. This strategic rotation allows teams to maintain proper court coverage, adapt to the picking up tips and off shots, and prepare for subsequent plays.

# COUNTER ROTATION

## VOLLEYBALL
### DEFENSE

# ADVANTAGES

1. Effective Blocking: Rotation defense excels in blocking at the net as blocking CROSS is highly efficient and easier to close.

2. Tip coverage: Able to pick up tips more efficiently as it pulls off blocker up for tips.

3. Effective Coverage: It provides good coverage against typical hit balls as it puts the best defenders in those coverage spots (line, cross, and cut).

4. Hide Bad defenders: If you have a setter that is poor at defense, then you can pull her up for tips instead.

# DISADVANTAGES

1. Spreads the defense: Counter Rotation defense can be susceptible to hard hits over the block as the backrow is spread out and their are bigger holes.

2. Out of system: The defense tends to put your team out of system on tips from OH or RH attack as your hitters will take the first contact and have to travel cross court to transition out for an attack.

3. Energy Demanding: As players have to move over long distances more often to get into position. Susceptible to quick sets.

4. Off blocker out of position: Off blockers are rotating to pick up tips, so they are not available to hit unless you have them run plays down the middle of the net or slides.

# COUNTER ROTATION DEFENSE

## Base (standard lineup):

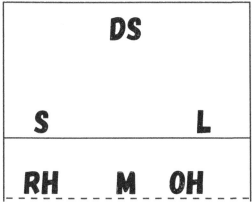

We are going to start in a standard base with setter back row. Don't release from base until the ball leaves the setters hands. The off blockers will move in more for tips in this defense.

## Defense against...

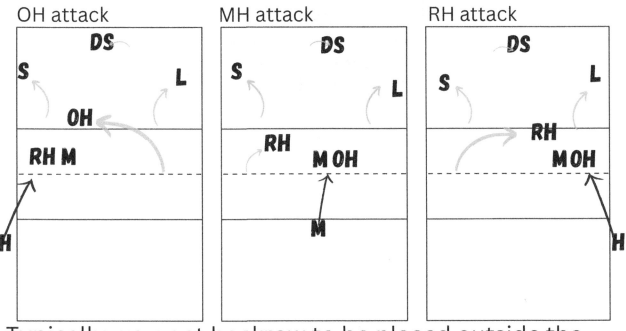

Typically we want backrow to be placed outside the block & between the block. If the block is closed then instead of between the block, then BR can read. Usually never behind the block.

# MAN UP

## VOLLEYBALL DEFENSE

# WHAT IS A MAN UP DEFENSE?

In a volleyball Man Up defense with a player pulled from the right back or middle back to the center of the 10-foot line, the team strategically reinforces their net defense against tips and short shots. By positioning this player at the ready to pick up tips, the defense gains an advantage in defending against opponents' finesse shots near the net. This adaptation enhances the overall blocking and digging capabilities, creating a formidable front-row defense against skillful attackers aiming to exploit short gaps in the court.

# MAN UP
## VOLLEYBALL
### DEFENSE

## ADVANTAGES

1. Less rotation movement: This defense is similar to rotation, but there is less movement as most players are within stepping distance in base.

2. Tip coverage: Able to pick up tips more efficiently against OH as it pulls someone (right back up for tips right away).

3. Effective Coverage: It provides good coverage against typical hit balls as it puts the best defenders in those coverage spots (line, cross, and cut).

4. Hide Bad defenders: If you have a setter that is poor at defense, then you can pull her up for tips instead. Or even pull up a middle back DS.

# MAN UP
## VOLLEYBALL
### DEFENSE

## DISADVANTAGES

1. Spreads the defense: Man up defense can be susceptible to hard hits over the block as as well as cut shots as the backrow is spread out and their are bigger holes.

2. Out of system: As the setter tends to be the one picking up tips, you will find your team out of system a bit more.

3. Less defenders against middle attack: Since these are typically quick you will have 2 people pick up tips and only 2 in the backrow for hard hits.

# MAN UP DEFENSE

## Base (Man up base with setter up):

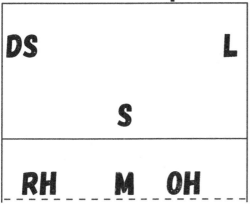

Start in a standard man up base with setter pulled up to the middle for tips and DS and L pulled back about 2 feet from endline. The off blockers will move back to cover pin attacks outside the block.

## Defense against...

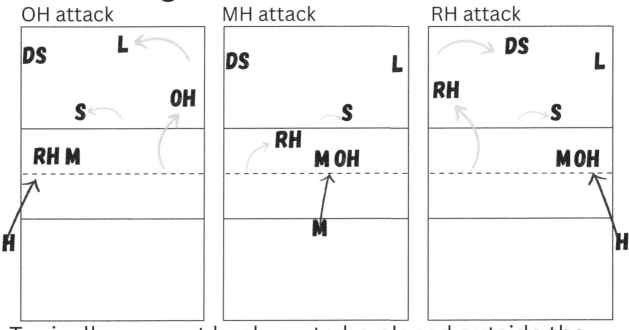

OH attack

MH attack

RH attack

Typically we want backrow to be placed outside the block & between the block.  If the block is closed then instead of between the block, then BR can read. Usually never behind the block.

# MIDDLE MIDDLE

# VOLLEYBALL DEFENSE

# WHAT IS A MIDDLE MIDDLE DEFENSE?

In a volleyball middle-middle defense, a player from the middle back position is shifted up to the center of the court, a location where many attacks tend to be directed. This strategic maneuver enhances the defense's readiness to handle powerful spikes and well-placed shots in the middle of the court. By positioning a player at this critical juncture, the team can more effectively counter the opponent's most frequent attacking area, improving their chances of digging, blocking, and transitioning into an offensive play.

# MIDDLE MIDDLE
## VOLLEYBALL
### DEFENSE

## ADVANTAGES

1. Effective Coverage: It was found that most of the balls are hit near the middle of the court so by putting someone in the middle your defense should be in position for most balls.

2. Minimal movement: The movement from base to defense is minimal as there is less movement, which will keep the team from being overworked.

3. Effective Seem Coverage: Since back row in middle middle is in a straighter line it is easier to read the seem balls and back up our teammates.

# MIDDLE MIDDLE
## VOLLEYBALL
### DEFENSE

## DISADVANTAGES

1. Susceptible to deep shots: Since are middle back is up in the middle, then our corners and endline are difficult to cover.

2. Susceptible to tips and dumps: Since our right back and left back players are 2 ft off the 10 ft line, then that leaves the team open to dumps and tips if they are NOT quick enough on the read.

3. Complexity : As a new defense, teams are NOT familiar and it may take the coach time to teach and effectively be able to run it effeciently.

# MIDDLE MIDDLE DEFENSE

## Base (middle middle base):

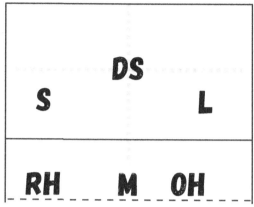

We are going to start with front row the same as usual, middle back (DS in this example) pulled to the middle of the back part of the court and right back (S) and left back (L) pulled about 2 ft from 10ft line and

## Defense against... sideline.

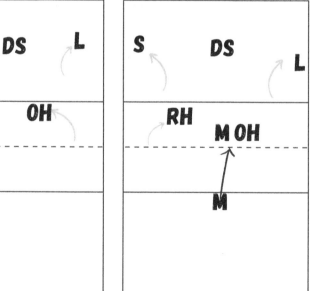

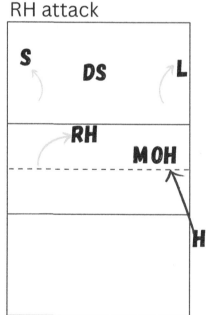

In this defense there is limited movement.  The person in middle back (DS), basically does NOT move  covers the middle of the court, use their hands for deep shots and BR person who is further from the ball will cover deep seem.

# HYBRID

## VOLLEYBALL
## DEFENSE

# WHAT IS A HYBRID DEFENSE?

A volleyball hybrid defense is a dynamic strategy that combines elements from two or more traditional defensive formations. By blending the strengths of different defenses, teams create a versatile and adaptable system. For example, combining a perimeter defense with elements of rotation or middle middle for different hitters can provide a comprehensive approach to handling various attack styles. Hybrid defenses allow teams to respond effectively to the complexity of modern volleyball, offering a diverse range of coverage options, block setups, and counter-attack strategies to confound opponents and maintain a strong presence on the court.

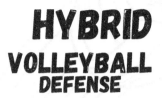

# HYBRID
## VOLLEYBALL
### DEFENSE

## ADVANTAGES

1. Versatility: Hybrid defenses allow teams to adapt to different situations during a match.

2. Play to teams strengths: Teams can strategically position players to match up against the most significant threats, improving the chances of success.

3. Flexibility: Coaches can adjust the defensive strategy during a match, making it harder for opponents to predict the defense and attack accordingly.

# HYBRID
## VOLLEYBALL
### DEFENSE

# DISADVANTAGES

1. Complexity: Implementing a hybrid defense can be challenging, requiring players to understand  principles effectively.

2. Communication: Effective communication is essential in hybrid defenses to ensure smooth transitions and player assignments.

3. Risk of Confusion: There is a risk of players becoming confused about their roles and responsibilities, leading to defensive breakdowns and open areas for opponents.

4. Dependent on Coaching Expertise: The success of a hybrid system relies heavily on the coach's ability to teach and implement the strategy effectively.

# HYBRID DEFENSE (EXAMPLE)

## Base (standard lineup):

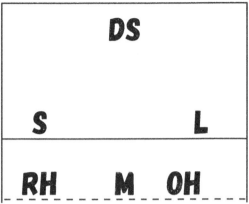

In this Hybrid example, we are going to start in a standard base with setter back row. Our plan here is to get our setter who is quick to get behind the block and help us pick up tips.

## Defense against...

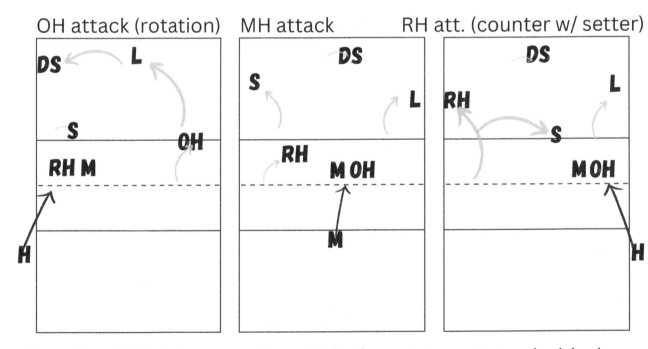

Here is a Hybrid system in which the setter rotates behind the block for tips. They Rotated for OH, and counter rotate with setter for RH. This is a good adjustment for a setter who is quick and can pick up tips but may not be a strong digger.

# KEY CONCEPTS:
# DEFENSE AGAINST OTHER MIDDLE ATTACKS

The next key concept is how to set up your defense against other middle attacks.  There are many different terminologies for this set in which some call it a 3-set or a "B" set to the middle.

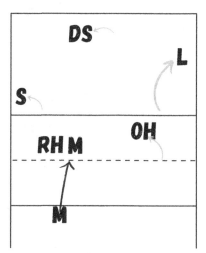

For the double block, your right side will come in, while your OH hitter will drop off for defense. Setter shifts up for tips and hits to sideline, DS shifts over to the seem of the block and left back (L) shifts back to outside of the block.

In conclusion, the world of volleyball defenses is a rich tapestry of strategies, each with its unique strengths and tactical intricacies. We've explored the precision of the perimeter, the adaptability of rotation, the teamwork in man-up formations, the agility in middle-middle structures, and the innovation of hybrid systems. As we close the final chapter, remember that mastering these defensive arts is not the destination but the journey itself. May this book serve as a guide and an inspiration for all those who find their place in the fascinating realm of volleyball defenses. The game is ever-changing, and with the knowledge you've acquired, you are well-equipped to rise to any challenge the court may present.

Made in the USA
Las Vegas, NV
16 December 2023

82889241R00031